I0160900

Australian Biographical Monographs

2

Australian Biographical Monographs
2

Harold Holt
and the liberal imagination

TOM FRAME

Connor Court Publishing

Published in 2018 by Connor Court Publishing Pty Ltd

Copyright © Tom Frame 2018

All rights reserved. No part of this book may be reproduced or transmitted in any form or by any means, electronic or mechanical, including photocopying, recording or by any information storage and retrieval system, without prior permission in writing from the publisher.

Connor Court Publishing Pty Ltd
PO Box 7257
Redland Bay QLD 4165
sales@connorcourt.com
www.connorcourt.com
Phone 0497-900-685

Printed in Australia

ISBN: 9781925501865

Front cover design: Maria Giordano
Front cover: Official visit to Arlington, Virginia (United States) by the Right Honourable Harold Edward Holt CH, Prime Minister of Australia, June 1966, hosted by the Honourable Robert McNamara, United States Secretary of Defense.
Source: Wikimedia Commons.

The principles which attracted me to the Liberal Party in the first instance are a truly Australian outlook, a determination to preserve for the Australian people freedom for the individual, opportunities and incentives for the individual, with emphasis on freedom of the individual.

These things have endured throughout the life of the party, and I believe these principles are the reason why we are attracting at this time so many young people either to our ranks or to our political support.

--Harold Holt, March 1966.

Introduction

It is intriguing to hear parliamentarians explain why they 'went into politics'. When conducting research fifteen years ago for a biography of Harold Edward Holt, Australia's seventeenth prime minister, I interviewed Holt's friends and foes including Sir Nigel Bowen and Dr Jim Cairns and asked about their motivations. Bowen entered Federal parliament and became a senior Coalition minister following a very successful legal career in Sydney including a term as president of the New South Wales Bar Council. After falling one vote short of securing the Liberal Party leadership at the end of 1972, he later became the first Chief Justice of the Federal Court of Australia. Jim Cairns pursued a very different path to Canberra. After service in the Victoria Police and an academic career, he was elected to parliament during the 1955 Labor split, narrowly losing a ballot for the leadership of the Labor Party in 1967 and rising to become Deputy Prime Minister in the Whitlam Government in 1974. Bowen and Cairns were known for firm and decided views about a range of issues.

In explaining why they sought political office, both unhesitatingly replied in altruistic terms: they wanted to make a difference to the quality of life enjoyed by their fellow Australians. Their personal and professional experiences had shaped their view of the public interest and how it was best served. Given these experiences diverged sharply, it was unsurprising that they offered contrasting views of what constituted the common good and the optimal strategies for securing it. Their competing political philosophies were clearly derived from the kinds of people and the character of events they had encountered. Their approach to government was also shaped by conceptions of what parliamentary processes and public administration could achieve. In sum, political imagination was shaped by personal convictions. By political imagination I mean a sense of what political processes could and should deliver for the Australian people in terms of fulfilling their needs and satisfying their wants, and what political institutions could and should achieve with a cogent vision of the future when coupled with resourceful leadership and able management.

Political imagination is critical to political effectiveness: it is the ability of elected representatives to form and then present mental images and word pictures of objects or outcomes not yet present or even considered possible to those they represent in the hope of eliciting their goodwill and enlisting their support. Imagination relies on creativity – the capacity to look into the future and to recognise the possibilities and potentialities that exist there. Imagination is not only recognising superior solutions to persistent problems it is seeing where a better future might lie and the clearest path to this fulfilment. Without imagination there is no vision. Where there is no vision there is no hope. Consequently, society is fractured by self-interest and there is a shift away from any sense of shared destiny. Imagination is integral to a holistic and healthy view of life and living. It is fundamental to the shaping of public life and the competing ideologies that parties present to the electorate and promote among voters. These parties consist of people whose beliefs are meant to coalesce around a policy platform, beliefs that are largely existential in character. Political leadership demands imaginative individuals blessed with creativity, intuition and insight. It also requires men and women whose life experiences have brought them into contact with people of different backgrounds. Those who have led a sheltered life or pursued a narrow career are best advised to think of another vocation. Politicians need to be well-rounded people who are self-aware and sensitive to difference.

A mature political philosophy is ideally one based primarily on personal convictions about human society. A well-developed philosophy touches on human origins and human purpose and draws on interpretations of human nature and conclusions about human flourishing. It explains the things of which people are made and the things for which they strive. I am describing what

David Kemp, the political scientist and former Howard Government minister, has called a 'leadership credo': 'what our political leaders have believed, and what their purposes and values have been'. It is a useful concept in that

> it puts the focus on the explicit and formulated ideas of political leaders as they face the choices that will lead to policy action. It is a key to understanding the meaning leaders give to the circumstances in which they find themselves, and their efforts to reconstruct these circumstances. It is the leader's credo that will be a key factor in determining whether an opportunity or pressure created by circumstances leads to a particular course of action.[1]

The existence of a credo makes the leader 'more understandable and predictable, and thus helps to remove one of the threatening uncertainties of leadership – what will the leader do next?'[2] There is a dynamic link between conviction and conduct which, for a popular leader, draws followers to the potential for participating in the realisation of a shared vision.

Because government is so pervasive in most Western societies, it is seen as integral to determining the quality of life enjoyed by those subject to its authority. The government can make the lives of citizens better and worse. It can make them richer and poorer; encouraging personal ambition and influencing individual decisions. But who decides when and how and where and why government will intervene in everyday life and shape the choices that people make about where they will invest their time and talent? In a democracy, it is those elected to public office who are empowered to legislate – to make laws that are intended to preserve peace and promote prosperity.

Parliamentarians are drawn from the general population and share many of the views held by the people. These views might not be held with the same force and effect but they will at least be present in discussions about policy and in debates about legislation. These same parliamentarians (other than independents) will also be required to imbibe their party's ideological commitments and, at least, publicly profess its formal opinions on a range of matters. This is an obligation of party membership and a function of group solidarity.

While contemporary Australian politics is derided for its unashamed pragmatism and, accordingly, denounced for its philosophical poverty, ideological battles based on competing visions of individual needs and prescriptions for human fulfilment were nonetheless prominent until the 1980s when election campaigns began to be fought on managerial competence and technical expertise. In effect, the decision to be made at election time has become which party is a better steward of the economy and more likely to secure the economic growth that delivers private affluence. Other than celebrity candidates, who secure pre-selection on the basis of their past sporting prowess or their media profile, a candidate's life experience does not appear to count for much in the eyes of either the political commentariat or the voting public. Regrettably, the range of a person's experiences and the quality of their reflection upon them does not receive any attention although both are critical to the evolution of their political philosophy and their capacity to be imaginative when in office. Democracies need people who have dealt with the hard questions that life sometimes poses.

Although there are few political dynasties in Australia – the Courts in Western Australia; the Creans in Victoria; the Downers in South Australia; the Hodgmans in Tasmania; the Katters in Queensland; and, the Anthonys in New South Wales – the political convictions and philosophical commitments of most candidates are now essentially subsumed by party platforms. Voters are rarely provided with an account of why a parliamentarian holds a particular view of a particular issue in terms of their practical acquaintance with the matters at hand. Because we live in an age that is more concerned with processes than principles, with implementation before ideas, a personal political philosophy is now usually acquired through membership of a registered party rather than discerned through careful and sustained assessment of lived experience and the successes and failures of previous legislators and administrators. The result is the preponderance of political sound bites, usually devoid of insight and wisdom, that essentially announce views without any reference to their origins. The superficiality of political dialogue and the enforced consensus that exists among professional politicians might also limit imagination and the enunciation of divergent political visions. But it has not always been this way. A previous generation thought and acted differently. An example is the nation's seventeenth prime minister, Harold Holt.

Holt was a conviction politician. He disliked ideologies because they were inflexible, providing solutions while usually being ignorant of the problems. Life provided the context for thinking and the textbook for ideas. Ready-made answers to policy problems seldom addressed the practical nuances of most questions. He was born in 1908 and experienced the disruption of the Great War of 1914-18. Harold was a sensitive child and was never indifferent to the world around him. He saw broken men and broken lives exacerbated by hardships inflicted during the Great Depression of 1929-32. The upheavals of his early life, including the separation of his parents and the early death of his mother, left him with an enlarged sympathy for those who suffered deprivations through no fault of their own. He was essentially a kind and compassionate man who wanted people to find and know happiness. Social ills needed to be addressed because they detracted from human contentment. If a compelling case could be developed, public and private resources should be invested in reducing suffering and eliminating despair. The future ought to be better than the past. Holt's work as a solicitor representing the business interests of clients, mainly in the fledgling entertainment industry, led him to oppose government regulation other than when and where it was unavoidable and plainly in the public interest. State sponsorship of any activity ought to be targeted and temporary because it was likely to become indiscriminate and permanent. Government was a blunt instrument that could not be applied with precision to achieve human happiness in many areas of life.

Beyond intrusive government programs and policies demanding compliance and conformity, Holt disliked coercion and compulsion of any kind. This included everything from curtailing the right to free association to mandatory trade union membership. These things infringed upon the liberties of citizens to make their own decisions and to determine the course of their own lives. As a young man eager to make his way in the world, he witnessed the titanic struggle between communism, fascism and democratic capitalism, and the factors and forces that led those around him to favour one over the other. In the turbulent 1930s it was impossible for a thinking person to be non-committal. The times demanded a stand between starkly different visions of human society and the role of the state in the regulation of human affairs. Strong convictions were almost inevitable because freedom and fraternity were at stake. Holt was clear: communism and fascism were two sides of an equally unacceptable political creed – totalitarianism. Such systems crush initiative and are a curse on imagination.

Although he demonstrated the genesis of a consistent political philosophy while an undergraduate at Melbourne University, Holt did not come from a politically active family and was not encouraged by his family to seek public office. He might just as easily have become a farmer or an entertainer given the vocations and occupations of those he knew in childhood and adolescence. Studying the law and becoming a lawyer suited his temperament. Having been raised by extended kin, boarding house tutors and the families of school friends, in adulthood he sought a more structured life that was marked by order and predictability. His love of the arts and sport brought him into contact with Melbourne's elite, including those associated with non-Labor politics. That he became active in party politics was unexpected but not surprising given the company he kept. Holt found himself increasingly alienated from conservatism and steadily attracted to liberalism. It was the place and importance of political imagination – of what was possible in terms of human advancement and individual fulfilment – that was the decisive factor in his professional mindset and one that remained a feature of his outlook when he eventually became prime minister.

Despite his standing as one of Australia's longest serving Federal politicians being a member of the House of Representatives for 32 years 125 days, Harold Holt has never been credited with making a substantial or lasting contribution to Australian political philosophy. He is often dismissed as a lightweight lacking intellectual gravitas and, surprisingly, political imagination. Portrayed as a political journeyman who outlasted his rivals, some observers contend he was without a defining success or an enduring legacy. He stood so long in Menzies' shadow, it has been suggested, that he was ill-suited to the exercise of political power when national leadership was handed to him. Much of this commentary reflects a low but inaccurate view of the six years between the retirement of Sir Robert Menzies in 1966 and the ascendancy of Gough Whitlam in 1972. As the prime ministers during this period. Holt is portrayed as unimaginative; John Gorton as ill disciplined; and, William McMahon as uninspiring although each made substantial contributions to national life – Holt foremost among the three.

Although well educated by the standards of the day, Holt did not study philosophy nor see himself as academically inclined. In terms of his personal disposition and professional outlook, he was principally a pragmatist whose first energies were devoted to getting things done that would improve the lives of ordinary Australians. He was not, however, bereft of ingenuity or lacking in creativity. He believed certain things about authority and power, institutions and processes and what parliaments could do to enhance opportunities for men and women. Holt was not so much pessimistic about government but realistic about the limits of its capacity. This assessment imparted a mood of modesty and a sanguine element to his political outlook.

In this sense he was not unlike his closest political friend beyond Australia, President Lyndon Johnson, although they were from opposing sides of the political spectrum. They first met in Melbourne in May 1942 and stayed in contact. Holt liked and admired Johnson. Shortly before he became the first United States' President to visit Australia, Johnson remarked:

> I know that government cannot resolve all these problems. It cannot make men happy or bring them spiritual fulfilment. But it can attempt to remedy the public failures which are at the root of so many of these human ills.[3]

Holt's approach was very similar. There are some things that government cannot do and should not even attempt to do. He thought it was morally wrong and politically suicidal to offer the electorate things that government could not deliver effectively or efficiently. It was the limits of government that shaped what passed as Harold's political philosophy and his judgements were shaped by long experience of being in power and being in opposition. His imagination was largely focussed on what the state could and couldn't do without intruding on the rights and freedoms, prerogatives and privileges of the people. The drawback with this thinking as he acquired more power and tried to preserve it was that problems tended to loom larger than solutions. He was too worried about inefficiency and too concerned with ineffectiveness. This meant his government attempted fewer things than it might and was inclined to risk aversion. Nevertheless, Holt implemented many new ideas and initiated a number of reforms that were not, and would never, have been contemplated by his predecessor. Most of these ideas and reforms are either overlooked or attributed to Holt's successors, including Labor Prime Minister Gough Whitlam. Although Holt is usually remembered as a rather 'grey man', he was fundamentally an imaginative man whose outlook reflected both the optimism and the prudence of classical liberalism.

****

This short book focuses on Harold Holt's political philosophy and its expression in what I have termed 'liberal imagination'. It is an attempt to show how a man of genuinely liberal instincts applied his initiative and creativity – the essence of imagination – to a range of political issues and practical challenges during the middle decades of the twentieth century. For Harold Holt the politician, the first question was always: is this a government responsibility? Answering 'yes' allowed a transition from principles to practicalities. If the answer was 'possibly' or even 'probably', the exercise of imagination was crucial because the decision to proceed involved an assessment of the future. Was government well placed to make a positive difference? Would government involvement serve the public interest and the common good or merely advance sectional interests and further private advantage? Could the application of public money require the imposition of unrealistic demands or unfavourable conditions on the intended beneficiaries? In the longer term, would government intervention improve or impede human flourishing or make the citizenry even more dependent on public intervention? Political parties, the press and the public rarely consider these questions of principal and practice in contemporary Australia. There is an implicit presumption that government intervention is always to be encouraged coupled with the assumption that money (the usual form of state intervention) can solve most problems if enough is provided. This widely held view is an abrogation of politics, a denial of liberal principles and a failure of imagination.

The life of Harold Holt provides some useful illustrations of political imagination and, later in his career, political stagnation. Notwithstanding the passage of fifty years, there is much to be learned from what Holt did and didn't do, and why. I have drawn some illustrative material from my 2005 work, *The Life and Death of Harold Holt*, but the interpretative dimension is new. I have chosen a series of incidents from his political career to illustrate the evolution of his political philosophy, the emergence of his liberal instincts and the exercise of his imaginative faculties. His approach to politics was not always consistent or even conscientious, after all, he had to secure votes and win elections. But the following pages will show that his dislike for ideology and disdain for compulsion not only increased his room to manoeuvre as a politician but encouraged the electorate to consider its rights and responsibilities within the broader body politic. At a time of increasing dependence on government and reliance on public assistance, there is much to commend in Holt's political liberalism and its contribution to human happiness.

Formative years

Harold Holt did not come from a politically active family. He was drawn to politics as a vocation by a small number of friends, most notably Robert Menzies who also functioned as his mentor. Associates and acquaintances thought Holt had the demeanour and the skills to become a legislator who could turn private aspirations into public policy. With the death of the Federal member for Fawkner, George Maxwell, in June 1935, Holt defeated a field of six candidates to win pre-selection for the United Australia Party (UAP), a political organisation founded by Labor dissidents and conservatives in 1931 to oppose Labor's economic program. It was not a party of firm or even decided political principles. It was essentially an anti-Labor coalition and this made it attractive to Holt but not the best 'fit' for his outlook on life.

Holt adopted what is now considered a characteristically 'Deakinite' position. He thought the UAP and Labor operated on the basis of very different philosophical outlooks. In campaigning for the Fawkner by-election in August 1935, Holt told the electorate that 'we must endeavour to find the relationship which lay somewhere between the complete non-interference of the last century and the complete interference of the Socialist State'. He said 'it was to be hoped that when the balance has been struck, a plan of economy would be attained without depriving man of his personal freedom, initiative, enterprise or the opportunities of his own development'. He thought that poverty existed because 'the problem of production had been solved but distribution was still a difficulty'. Holt advocated support for housing-unemployment schemes, slum reclamation and a national unemployment insurance scheme. When asked by the local press to describe his political aspirations, Holt said:

> My own interest in politics arises from the conviction that this is a political age, whereas the nineteenth century, occupied with problems of industrial production and expansion, was a scientific age. Today the problems are social and political – securing an effective use of those productive forces which a century of scientific endeavour produced and the equitable distribution of their product. My support for this particular party arises from the conviction that it is the one party which does aim at legislating for the community as a whole and not for one particular class.

Holt polled well. He gained 24,594 votes to the Labor candidate's 16,433. There were predictions that Maxwell's majority of 14,922 would be cut to 5,000. Holt's majority was 8,151. Despite the local popularity of the previous member and the customary general swing away from the government party in a by-election, Holt managed to maintain much of the

UAP's majority. The Party was pleased with its newest and youngest parliamentarian whose electorate took in the prestigious Melbourne suburbs of South Yarra, Toorak, Prahran, Armadale and Windsor.

Holt's early public speeches were solid and workmanlike. Still a political novice, he enunciated no grand vision for Australia or its people. There was no 'New Deal' or 'Great Society' that he longed to create. But he believed in the virtue of hard work and frugality; the importance of expanding opportunity for individuals and business; and, avoiding the over-regulation of the economy and unnecessary intrusion into social life. Notably, he did have some decidedly liberal – meaning progressive – views that he never abandoned. In some respects, his outlook was somewhat bohemian. Although he lived a fairly conventional life, he believed that people were entitled to live unconventional lives and to pursue their dreams and aspirations however alternative and avant-garde they might seem to others. His appreciation of the visual and dramatic arts and his eclectic taste in music and sport, meant he could appreciate and empathise with those who wanted to live differently to the mainstream. Holt argued for changing Australia's immigration laws to grant equal opportunity for women to become citizens, for more women to enter parliament and for divorce law reform that was more favourable to women. Holt also lobbied for the National Fitness campaign, advocated by the

Age newspaper, to become a government priority. He pointed out to Prime Minister Lyons that the British government had invested in the program he was supporting. He was subsequently appointed to the Coordinating Council for Physical Fitness and promoted its programs as public encouragement of private choice.

Holt had strong views on other subjects and was prepared to express them. The first instance was when he voted with the Opposition when the Government attempted to avoid answering a question on the constitutional crisis created by King Edward VIII's decision to marry the American divorcee, Wallis Simpson. He felt the matter needed to be discussed and drafted his own question for parliament the next day. Although the youngest parliamentarian, he was willing to make his mark by widening political sentiment at least within his own party.

Political progress

Holt's mentor, Robert Menzies, became Prime Minister in April 1939. Recognising his energy and ability, Menzies immediately appointed him 'Minister without Portfolio', a post he held until the following year when he enlisted in the Australia Army and trained for overseas service with the 2/4ᵗʰ Field Regiment. He was recalled to Cabinet in October 1940 as Minister for Labour and National Service and concurrently Minister-in-Charge of Scientific and Industrial Research. The most lasting of Holt's achievements in this period was the introduction of universal child endowment.

In January 1941, Cabinet decided to introduce child endowment of five shillings for each child under the age of 16 years (after the first) regardless of family income. This was a means of assisting families at a time when the wartime adjustment of award wages threatened to fall with undeserved severity on family groups. Although it was customary for legislation of this significance to be introduced by the Prime Minister or a senior Cabinet Minister, the Treasurer, Arthur Fadden, 'passed the responsibility to Harold as I felt it would be to his great advantage to be associated at this stage of his career with such a major measure'.[4]

Holt promoted the scheme as a 'foretaste and pledge of the full reconstruction that will be possible when we can again turn our surplus productive forces to the purposes of peace'.[5] Holt told the readers of the *Australian Women's Weekly*:

> I don't need to tell any housewife coping with her household budget these days how much that extra £1 [for five children] a week will be. We are determined that this endowment money will be spent expressly on the maintenance and upbringing of the child. For this reason payments will be made to the mother or to the person directly responsible for the child's care.[6]

The *Child Endowment Act* was passed in April 1941. The press praised Holt's initiative and creativity. He was not pressed to consider the legislation. While the need was apparent, fulfilling it was the principal question. The 'only bachelor in Federal Parliament' was now referred to as the 'Godfather to 1,000,000 Australian children'. Labor Opposition leader John Curtin said in the House of Representatives: 'I am sure that the House would like some expression of appreciation, and, indeed, of admiration for the Minister for the labour he has expended on this bill and for the notable place which this monumental legislation will give him in the annals of this federation'. Holt was rightly proud of his achievement because it was targeted state support designed to achieve a specific outcome – the improved nurture of children. But the UAP-Country Party minority government, of which Holt was a member, only lasted until October 1941 when two independents crossed the floor and the Labor Party formed government.

In his 1943 election campaign speech, Holt complained of Australia being 'the highest taxed country in the world' and lamented the 'degree of industrial unrest [which was] unrivalled in any other part of the globe'. He went on to highlight Communist control of trade unions and their access to funds for the purpose of political agitation. Labor was, he said, 'a defeatist party with an outmoded ideology'. In reply, the Sydney *Telegraph* said that Holt, 'who has fundamentally liberal instincts, has been spoiled and has mentally run to fat'.[7] Holt retained his seat but, as expected, the Curtin Government was returned to office. The UAP's parliamentary ranks were devastated. Labor had won 49 seats and commanded a substantial majority. The UAP won just 12 of the 74 House of Representative seats and had lost its majority in the Senate where Labor had won all nineteen seats contested. Holt was one of few pointing to any positive outcomes for the non-Labor side in the election result. He said it had

> proved a death blow to the die-hard Tories. It has also been a UAP Dunkirk but if due heed were taken of the lessons it taught, the setback would be in the interests of the party. It was only by a revolutionary

> change in outlook and the adjustment of policies
> to the great problems of today that the party could
> give the people effective leadership … there were
> some elements of good in Labor's policy, and the
> UAP answer must not be die-hard Toryism; it
> needed liberalism in its spirit and democracy in its
> organisation.

Holt imagined a new party rather than a reformed UAP. Menzies regained the UAP leadership on 23 September 1943 but worked immediately for its demise with the support of people like the member for Fawkner. A conference held in Albury from 14-16 December 1944 settled on the principles upon which the new Liberal Party would be founded. Holt was not a major practical contributor to the formation of the new organisation although he was the first to join the Prahran branch of the Liberal Party after its formation on 8 February 1945. Menzies announced in the House of Representatives on 21 February 1945 that the main Opposition party would from henceforth be known as the Liberal Party.

At the inaugural meeting of the Party in northern Tasmania one month later, Holt spoke of a cleavage between the Government and the non-Labor forces,

> between the ideals of a Government which sought
> to drug the nation with talk of social service and
> the ideals of all those who still believe in personal
> initiative, in individual risk-taking for the sake of

the commensurate rewards and in the principles of private enterprise … It is because that cleavage is so plain that we must sink our party and personal differences and unite the people who think as we do.[8]

The outlook of the new party was an attempt at genuine liberalism and it was an organisation in which Holt was much more at home. He said:

We share the broad policy objectives of Labor – a steadily rising standard of living, encouragement and development of effort by the individual. However, the Socialist approach will impede rather than assist those objectives. Actually between Labor and my party there is a difference of method, not of objective. The difference is between the regimented State and the State in which the emphasis rests on the individual.

In a speech delivered during the August 1945 by-election for the seat of Fremantle made vacant by John Curtin's death, Holt said the Liberal Party policy stands for 'the 'four decencies': a good job, a home, adequate social security and an expanded educational service'.[9] Notably, the Liberals were not promising specific outcomes but opportunities that would create an environment in which human dignity would be enhanced and human happiness would be enlarged.

With the Second World War over and the Liberal Party attempting to consolidate its political standing,

Holt became the Opposition spokesman on immigration and industrial relations. He attempted to embrace a genuinely liberal rather then a merely conservative attitude towards both portfolios and appeared to have a sound grasp of the defining issues. Holt conceded that 'some unrest in industry is a continuing condition just as it is in human beings and in human affairs ... unrest in industry has redressed many an evil and produced a progressive improvement in working conditions'.[10] He distinguished between strikes and lock-outs, and between good and bad workers and bosses. But he felt the greatest problem was the politicisation of the trade union movement and its virtual marriage to the Labor Party, and that many strikes were not about wages or conditions but a wider attack on society by Communists. 'Their aggressiveness is accentuated in Australia by their Communist leadership of the coalmining, stevedoring and seamen's unions'. He quoted from Communist union leader Ernie Thornton and 'Comrade L Sharkey', President of the Communist Party, in claiming that Communist dominance of trade unions was assisted by rank and file apathy, and by the exploitation of mateship – 'one of the virtues in our national character'. He also restated the 'four decencies' of Liberal policy: a decent home, job, employment for children and program of social benefits. Yet he feared that Australia was drifting towards a 'New Anarchy' resulting from an inadequate political expression of

the economic basis of our society'. He said: 'Australian politicians fall into two broad groups, one comprising the members of the Labor Party pledged to a socialist program, and the other comprising non-Labor parties advocating private enterprise'.

There was also anarchy within trade unions caused by open conflict between Communist and non-Communist factions. The politicisation of labour relations meant that political power rested in the hands of those who were not accountable to the electorate. This was particularly egregious in relation to foreign affairs where left-wing unions were black-banning ships from the Netherlands bound for the Dutch East Indies where an anti-Imperial struggle was underway. He observed that 'the Government opposes the bans, the ACTU disapproves of them but the ships are not loaded'. 'The question facing the nation', he said, 'was whether the Government can and should regulate the activities of trade unions or allow them to operate as an irresistible pressure group'. He commented that Australia has a 'strongly entrenched tradition against the use by governments of military forces to break a strike'. He attempted to articulate a moderate view of labour relations more generally: 'The employer must foster a sense of purpose and pride of achievement in his worker. The worker must recognise the unceasing difficulties of conducting a business on a profitable basis in a competitive world'. This meant 'exploding the doctrine of the class war. We must reveal the baselessness of a so-called 'right to strike'".

It was clear that industrial disputes were directly affecting the nation's economic performance while the Chifley Government seemed incapable of curbing militant unionism. Holt directed most public attention to what he considered Labor's socialist agenda. He attacked the Shipping Bill in which the Government proposed establishing a Commonwealth shipping line and developing an Australian shipbuilding industry because he was critical of the poor performance of the Australian Shipping Board and the domination of the waterfront by the Communist-led Waterside Workers' Federation. He claimed the Banking Bill, which would empower the Commonwealth Bank to lay down policy on trading bank credit advances, was actually an attack on private enterprise. Holt argued that excessive government participation and regulation of industry and manufacturing led to diminished private investment, inflation and recession. Holt said that 'small businesses are the large companies of the future. They need not only profits that can be ploughed back, but if they are to grow they will require additional capital. Their need is not for government loans but venture capital that enters the business as a partner for profit or loss'. He argued that the Government's role was that of an enabler. It needed to promote political stability, confidence in the policies of the administration, a tax-scale which gives incentives for risk-taking, an acceptable industrial code which will ensure continuity of work and will be applied with authority, and a minimum of government interference in industry. Public works may have a limited usefulness as a stop-gap programme while production arising from private investment is being developed.[11]

Holt was also critical of the persistent shortage of basic goods, particularly petrol, and the continuation of rationing, and the over-extension of government activity. He asserted that 30 per cent of the total national production was passing through the hands of the Chifley Government for activities that had no useful purpose in peacetime. Holt claimed that Labor had deliberately worked to reduced the prestige and authority of the Federal Parliament by transferring critical financial functions to a supreme economic council that had 'become a mere recording instrument for the one man who dominated it – Mr Chifley'.[12]

The nation went to the polls on 10 December 1949. The election was a poll on Labor policies, principally bank nationalisation. Prime Minister Chifley wanted to bring all of the banks under Commonwealth Government control. The Coalition was determined to oppose the policy while bringing an end to the persistence of wartime rationing. A crippling coal strike and the escalating Cold War led to real fears of communist domination at home and abroad. At a political rally at the Melbourne Town Hall, Holt told the audience not to 'be misled by Ben Chifley's Irish charm and humour, because there is no more fanatical Socialist in the Federal cabinet'.[13] Holt attacked Labor for high-taxes and big government spending. He said the Liberals would 'repeal the 1947 *Bank Nationalisation Act* and seek to include in the Constitution a provision making such a Socialist monopoly impossible without the approval of the people expressed by referendum'.[14] Holt attacked the Labor Party for not putting Communists last on their 'How to Vote' cards in some electorates or for giving Communists their preferences ahead of all other non-Labor parties. He asserted that the Coalition had 'undertaken to deal with Communism as an enemy within our gates. To do so they will need the backing of every loyal Australian'.[15]

Holt warned his own party that 'the next three years might be the Liberal Party's last real chance to establish itself as the alternative to Labor ... There is a serious danger of Liberalism being forced to extreme right and the political contest of the future resolving itself into a struggle between the right and left wings of labour. English Liberalism – a driving force a generation ago – is virtually extinct'. Holt was adamant that more than just 'a swing of the pendulum is needed to place the Party in power'. The election outcome was a strong

victory to the Coalition which won 55 seats and the Country Party 19 to Labor's 47. In the Senate, the Coalition won 23 of the contested seats to Labor's 19. The Labor Party had lost office but retained a majority in the Senate – the last time it would ever do so.

The Governor-General, William (later Sir William) McKell, swore in the new Menzies' ministry on 19 December 1949. As expected, Holt was given the two senior portfolios of Labour and National Service and Immigration. The 'twinning' of the two departments under one minister highlighted the connection between immigration and the needs of the labour market. The influential *Smith's Weekly* remarked that 'no man in the whole Cabinet team is better suited than Holt to the task allotted him'.[16] Holt now ranked fourth in Cabinet and was riding high. In his electorate Christmas message, Holt claimed that: 'a decisive political battle has been fought and won, and we can feel justly proud, as a people, of the good humour and calm consideration that was given, with few exceptions, so generally displayed on the great issues of the campaign. But that now lies behind us, and part of the responsibility of the new Government is to weld the Australian people more closely together'.[17] It was now time for Holt's considerable political potential and his liberal imagination to be translated into a solid parliamentary and ministerial performance.

Imaginative immigration

Although Cabinet set the broad policy parameters, the minister was given discretion to interpret and implement the Coalition's immigration policy in relation to specific cases brought before him. Holt took this discretion to its limits and displayed a genuine liberal spirit and an imaginative approach. His long-term aim was to increase the initial target of 70,000 migrants per year to 200,000 primarily from Britain, Holland, Malta and Ireland with the goal of increasing Australia's population to 9 million by 1953.[18] The initial goal was annual population growth of 3 per cent throughout the coming decade. Although there was a preference for British migrants and families, Holt extended the policy of accepting non-British migrants to cope with those displaced by the war and the post-war Soviet occupation of Eastern Europe and the need for single male workers for major public works such as the Snowy Mountains Hydro-Electric Scheme. The main impediment to achieving the desired number was lack of housing. Government hostels were in demand and the standard of accommodation was in need of improvement although far superior to what most had known in Europe.

The new Opposition leader, Dr HV Evatt, led the former immigration minister, Arthur Calwell, and a number of anti-Communist Labor parliamentarians in attacking the Government and Holt as Immigration Minister in particular for allowing a delegation of five Australians to participate in a 'peace meeting' at Peking in May 1952 while the Korean War was in progress. The political feeling generated by the Labor attack led the Government to reverse its position and refuse passports to a larger group who wanted to attend another major conference in Peking that had been planned by delegates at the May meeting.[19] In a letter to fellow communist Stephen Murray-Smith, prominent intellectual Brian Fitzpatrick wrote that Holt confided that he 'had misgivings about the policy but felt that he could do nothing in the prevailing atmosphere … he said to kick the Left in such a fashion is bad practice, as the boot may one day be on the other foot'.[20] Holt told the Press that he was, however, 'amazed' by the strength of protests directed against him for refusing passports to individuals wanting to travel abroad for potentially subversive activities. He pointed out that requests from individuals who might constitute a security risk for a passport were considered by the intelligence services. But Holt maintained that 'the right to travel is a very important one and should be jealously guarded and not be subject to arbitrary determination by any government. It would require a strong security recommendation to me against the issue of a passport before I would refuse one'.

But the passport controversy would not go away. The Australia people were yet to be persuaded by the Government's case for restricting their right to travel and free association. Holt privately agreed with the public's view. Notwithstanding the defection of the Soviet diplomat Vladimir Petrov in April 1954, by March 1955 the electorate had become less sympathetic to the Government's refusal to grant passports to alleged 'Reds' to attend what it referred to as 'so-called Peace Conferences'. The turning point proved to be Holt's refusal to grant a passport to the Reverend Neil Glover, the vicar of St Matthias Church in Richmond, Victoria and an executive member of the Australian Peace Council, to attend a conference of the World Peace Movement in Helsinki in May 1955. When Holt was lobbied by a number of senior Anglican churchmen and still refused, Glover threatened to take the matter to the High Court. On 6 April and after prevailing against some of his party colleagues, Holt announced that the Government would apply a policy of practically unrestricted issue of passports. He explained that the Korean War had ended, the conflict in Indochina had not yet escalated into a regional conflict and that the special restrictions following Petrov's defection could be eased. Glover was granted a passport and another damaging controversy was averted. Holt's achievement was to calm the fears of his parliamentary colleagues and party officials who often imagined the worst could and would happen.

In the seven years he administered the Immigration Department, Holt maintained Calwell's better initiatives with more than Calwell's tact and diplomacy.[21] In fact, there was remarkable consistency in immigration policy between Labor and the Coalition with few discontinuities. The difference was that while Holt said publicly he upheld the policy of mostly white European immigration, he had already begun to dilute and erode it by the generous application of ministerial discretion. Holt relaxed the policy through changes to the eligibility requirements for citizenship: extending eligibility for citizenship to non-European spouses of European immigrants; allowing the non-European wives of Australian servicemen to become Australian citizens; the admission of immediate relatives as Australian citizens and the grant of indefinite work permits to allow qualified people to remain in the country and to allow non-European immigrants resident in Australia for fifteen or more years to become citizens.[22] After Holt took office, 'with the exception of a few minor cases, the 1950s were almost entirely free of incidents related to the White Australia policy. Most Australians, due very largely to Holt's more flexible attitude to the subject and new immigration legislation enacted in 1956 and 1957, believed that the general tenor of the policy was changing'.[23] Holt presented a caring and humane public face, and won for himself and the Liberal Party personal and electoral popularity with non-British migrants.

Holt was asked to nominate his greatest success after seven years as Immigration Minister. It was, he said, preventing conservative elements in his party from winding back the immigration program. In his final contribution to the magazine *The Good Neighbour*, Holt spoke strongly of:

> The necessity to avoid destroying carefully cultivated good relations with emigration countries and the need to maintain the confidence of governments, investors and others both within Australia and overseas to emphasise the desirability of avoiding both any permanent reduction in what is deemed the manageable rate of immigration and a major cut in the programme ... a continuation of a high level of immigration can ensure the continuation of this progress which will bring in its train improved productivity and other benefits arising from larger scale activity. The simple fact is that immigration is one major influence that leaves the country with a long-term asset on both political and economic grounds.[24]

He relinquished the Immigration portfolio on 24 October 1956 shortly after he became Deputy Leader of the Liberal Party and Leader of the House of Representatives.

Imaginative industrial relations

Harold Holt was given the portfolio largely because he was the Liberal minister most acceptable to moderate elements in the labour movement. This endorsement was not because trade union leaders thought he was weak or pliable but because he understood their concerns and possessed sound negotiation skills. Holt was open to creative proposals and imaginative solutions to enduring industrial problems. He also believed in state regulation of the labour market, and thought an unfettered labour market was both inefficient and contrary to the specific needs of the post-war Australian economy which required government direction rather than domination. Holt's parliamentary colleague, Jo Gullett, remarked: 'Harold's greatest quality was the ability to see and sympathise with other points of view. This is very laudable in a politician. It meant that for a start he was generally liked and respected in the Parliament, regardless of party. It also meant that he had developed very good relations with the trade union leaders'.[25] According to Holt, the industrial challenges facing the Menzies-Fadden Government when it took office included 'Communist control of key industrial unions; a weakened arbitration system lacking effectively disciplinary powers; a hostile Senate, making substantial legislative amendment difficult, if not impracticable; a suspicious and uncooperative attitude on the part of the Trade Union movement'.[26] Holt believed the last challenge was foremost and offered the key to improved industrial relations. He worked hard at establishing and maintaining a close relationship with Albert Monk, the President of the Australian Council of Trade Unions (ACTU).

Political correspondent Alan Reid praised Holt for his 'successful resistance of pressure from his own Party' to attack trade unions and noted the personal support he had from Menzies and Fadden who trusted Holt's judgement.[27] He had earlier told the Liberal Federal Executive that there was a tendency within the Party to 'over-dramatise the effect and incidence of strikes' and to side too readily and hastily with the side of the employer.[28] But Holt was already being accused by some within the Liberal Party of being an 'appeaser'. Monk's close relationship with Holt provoked some unionists to side with Communists in the labour movement rather than moderates, as Monk was depicted. Holt wanted to eradicate Communist influence in trade unions but did not want to damage the labour movement as a whole. His moderate stance was not just charting a course between equally unattractive extremes but finding a way forward that was effective, efficient and, most importantly, one that attracted a sustainable consensus and continuing support.

Holt attempted a number of other reforms that tackled illiberal elements of industrial relations. The Secret Ballots Bill was drafted to prevent further Communist infiltration of unions and to preclude Communist intimidation of workers. Communists active in the Amalgamated Engineering Union (AEU) challenged the legislation in October 1953. Holt said the Liberal Party 'always believed that if a faithful expression could be given by democratic means to the wishes of rank-and-file unionists, they would speedily put an end to Communist influence in their midst'.[29] Holt also resisted the imposition of compulsory unionism in New South Wales. He told the Federal Council of the Liberal Party that it was 'detestable', that it 'indicated the fascist turn of mind' in the Labor Party and was contrary to United Nations and International Labour Organisation (ILO) declarations. He also urged unions to remain with the Commonwealth Arbitration Court rather than moving to State tribunals or other processes of collective bargaining (such as direct negotiation with employers) following the Court's decision on 28 October 1953 to suspend automatic quarterly basic wage adjustments and replace them with annual adjustments based on economic performance and productivity. The Court argued that the economy was stable and could not increase wages without affecting costs and prices. Employer organisations had wanted to increase hours and decrease pay in order to maintain economic stability. Holt defended the Court's decision by pointing out that it had previously shortened the working week and increased the basic wage. Holt also turned on the relationship between unions and the Labor Party saying it was too close and damaged potentially harmonious negotiations with employers. However, he welcomed ALP control of the AEU as a 'stinging rebuff to the Communists'.

Holt's success in managing Australian industrial relations was recognised internationally. He attended the International Labour Conference (ILO) in June 1957. The ILO was formed as a result of the Treaty of Versailles. Holt hosted the first ILO event held in Australia – a conference on pneumoconiosis (diseases of the lungs arising from inhalation of dust) at Sydney University in early 1950. In his welcome speech, Holt said:

> Labour problems – problems of industry have always in Australia occupied a position of very great importance ... the work of the ILO enjoys the support of the responsible political bodies in Australia, irrespective of the change of governments from time to time ... the Government which I have the honour to represent has already given thought to the question of increasing Australia's representation at future meetings of the ILO.[30]

Holt was also the first Australian Minister for Labour to take part in an ILO conference. He attended as a 'Visiting Minister' in 1953. Incidentally, the 1953 conference discussed the admission of the Republic of China's (Taiwan) admission. There were 115 votes in favour (including Australia), 29 against and 47 abstentions. Holt made no reference to the problem of representation in his address at the Plenary session. Two years later, Australia supported moves to allow Taiwan to vote. It was passed with Australia's support in 1955. By the time of the 1957 conference, there were representatives from 73 countries and a total membership of 800 delegates and advisers. The focus on the 1957 gathering was the effects of automation and two conventions on forced labour and providing for a 24-hour rest period every week. Holt was elected to the Presidency of the Conference after being proposed by the Government delegations of Thailand, Chile and France, the workers delegation of Canada, and the employers' delegation of France. There were no other nominations. Claude Jodoin, the Canadian workers' delegate, said in support of Holt's nomination: 'We of the workers group know of the Right Honourable Harold Holt by reputation, and we know that he has always looked upon the requests of the workers of this country with much sympathy. We are sure that through the experience he has acquired, and his loyalty to the ILO, he will certainly be an excellent President'. In his presidential address, Holt said that:

Few nations can insulate themselves against what
is happening in other countries. The work of this
Organisation, therefore, can not only benefit those
countries whose living standards are comparatively
low ... but can also help other advanced countries
... It has become fashionable to gaze into the
crystal ball of the future. According to their
political outlook some see a world of capitalism,
some a world of communism. I believe that if
all governments were to direct themselves to the
objectives [of social justice and national security],
they will find themselves increasingly drawn into
a partnership with management and labour in
which these differences tend to diminish. I would
describe this process as a dynamic and progressive
liberalism ... based on this conception of a
harmonious cooperative partnership between these
three essential elements in the modern State.

This left no room for class warfare but plenty of
scope for incentive. Holt said that 'no country attaches
more importance to matters which are of concern to
the ILO, such as the cultivation of good industrial
relations and the establishment of international
cooperation for these purposes'.[31] He observed that
'those of us in this conference who have laboured over
the years for better relations in industry know that when
we find a clash of extremes, we must usually evolve a
middle way to produce the desired agreement'.[32] In his
closing remarks Holt said: 'I shall go back to my own
public duties not merely enriched with a great deal of

knowledge but understanding, I believe, rather better the point of view of peoples from so many diverse parts of the earth and holding so many diverse points of view, not all of which would necessarily coincide with my own'.[33]

In the Government's first year in office more than 2,000,000 days were lost through industrial disputes. Eight years later, the figure had declined to 439,000 working days. During Holt's ministerial tenure, the number never reached 1.5 million in a calendar year and did not exceed one million working days in four of the previous eight years. While Holt's leadership had been a factor, general economic conditions, the growth of hire-purchase commitments among low-income groups, the gradual trend away from political militancy towards legal remedies in many unions also contributed to his success. Key unionists were also given a direct means of influencing government policy. Holt explained:

> For many years I have tried to set up a body which would be representative of the Government and of top management, and the Trade Unions so that we could sit around the table together and discuss ... national economic problems where we can combine together for the national good. [The Ministry of Labour Advisory Council was the result.] We have already examined such questions as the employment of the older aged, the physically disabled, safety in industry, the provision of a work

> force in the seasonal industries; and … the problems
> which a full employment situation creates for us.[34]

Political commentator Don Whitington judged Holt's years in Labour and National Service his most productive in public life:

> He brought to the task a humanity, a tolerance, a
> moderation and a willingness to compromise that
> contributed greatly to the comparative harmony
> that prevailed for most of his term of office. The
> country was never as free of industrial trouble as
> while Holt held the portfolio – in what normally
> could have been stormy post-war years. The
> communists were at the zenith of their peace
> time strength in the unions; there was an extreme
> Right wing faction in the Cabinet that wanted a
> showdown with the unions at any cost, and there
> was a considerable body of opinion in the rank
> and file of the coalition parties that would have
> supported such tactics.[35]

Holt was able to deal with the fears of employers and employees because his approach to industrial relations was liberal and imaginative. A solution that suited one side at the expense of the other was not a sustainable solution. It provided the seeds of the next conflict. Holt needed to think 'outside the square' and beyond the confines of a narrow ideological approach to managing workplace tensions. He argued that workers ought to 'put pressure on inefficient and slipshod employers' in order to improve production output and raise standards of living.[36] Holt spoke at the official opening of the new ACTU building in Carlton on 30 June 1954 and said: 'no Australian Government, whatever its policy, could deal with great national problems without closely collaborating with the trade union movement'.[37] Holt publicly acknowledged the role of the trade unions in accepting immigrants and even commended the more militant unions at the Port Kembla and Newcastle steelworks where nearly ten per cent of the workers were displaced persons. He also recognised that the influx of people fleeing from communism in Europe was disinclined to vote for a party that had been labelled pro-Communist.

Holt believed that the ACTU did not need to ally itself formally with the Labor Party because an enlightened government could ensure that capital and labour existed harmoniously. With the prospect of full employment and increasing wages, this was possible. The *Age*'s editor and later Holt's speechwriter, Keith Sinclair, noted Holt's 'great success was to accommodate conflicting spirits and people in the industrial movement'.[38] He formed close and continuing friendships with ACTU officials, especially Albert Monk. His relations with Jim Healy of the Waterside Workers Federation remained cordial and constructive even when they were locked in a bitter dispute. He also worked well with the courts. Sir Richard Kirby, President of the Arbitration Commission, said of the years after

Holt left the Labour portfolio: 'It was as useful as having Bill the cat as Minister. The Government put coves in the job who didn't have a clue. I'd see their eyes gazing as I tried to explain things – they literally could not understand what industrial relations was about'.[39] Looking back, Holt said: 'I believe for the first time since Federation we did produce some thawing of the frozen attitudes between management and labour'.[40] His liberal imagination had prevailed.

Holt relinquished the Labour and National Service portfolio on 10 December 1958 after nearly nine years in office.

The state and the market

As a classical liberal, Holt believed in small government and trusted in market mechanisms other than when the economy needed government intervention to overcome external distortions and periodic aberrations. Although wartime rationing had ended and a number of large government funded public works were underway, Holt thought an election held at the end of 1952 would lead to 'a land slide to Labor' because the Government had not done enough to support economic growth. Too little had been done to impart continuing momentum to infrastructure development and industrial expansion. A doctrinaire approach that left everything to the market or private initiative was unhelpful in the shadow of the Second World war and the global instability reflected in the outbreak of the Korean War in June 1950. He felt there was little time to 'stage a recovery' before the May 1953 half-Senate election. Holt argued that the Government's problems were obvious. The first and most severe was inflation. The electorate blamed the Government and would hold it accountable. The second problem was the re-emergence of unemployment for the first time in a decade. Holt commented that 'the fear of unemployment has undoubtedly affected many who supported us both in 1949 and 1951'. And the problem was bound to get worse.

> The political effects flowing from this decline in
> the employment level need no stressing. We will all
> be aware that for every person unemployed, there
> are friends, relatives and fellow workers who react
> to the unemployment of the person out of work.
> In the months ahead political considerations will be
> of far more consequence than the economic. Our
> policy of diverting labour to the basic industries
> has been realised ... We no longer have a 'milk
> bar' economy. Rather we have an economy of 'all
> dressed up and no place to go'. We must be prepared
> to make a realistic appraisement of the political
> consequences of a continuance or aggravation of
> the current rate of unemployment.[41]

There were no precise solutions or new initiatives. Holt simply wanted his colleagues to realise the seriousness of the party's plight before deciding on any form of intervention. Treasury produced a 'diversion' entitled 'Proposals for Specific Action to Maintain and Stimulate Employment' which included some modest proposals for placing defence supply orders with local industry. It was clear that the Treasury hoped to maintain existing policy and hope the threat of recession would recede. The electorate expected the Government to deliver an economic boom even as it was fearful of another depression. Holt was frustrated by the Government's lack of imagination and creativity. It seemed bereft of genuinely enticing new ideas and the only thing that prevented it from losing office was the electorate's unwillingness to restore Labor to power so soon.

A liberal ascendency?

On 1 December 1954, Robert Menzies became Australia's longest serving prime minister. Including his first term as prime minister (1939-41), he had been in office for 7 years and 106 days when he surpassed the previous record set by Billy Hughes. Talk of succession naturally gained momentum. Journalist Rohan Rivett reported in 1954 that Menzies wanted Holt as 'they represent the liberal, middle of the road section of the party and in most major matters of policy are more broadminded and progressive than the majority of the benches behind them. As the whole electoral tendency since the war has been towards a mild, genuinely liberal policy, the Menzies-Holt outlook tends to gain ground at the expense of a more diehard and illiberal philosophy'.[42] But Holt was still ranked fourth in Cabinet. The succession would become clearer when there was a ballot for the position of Deputy Party Leader when Sir Eric Harrison, the incumbent since the Liberal Party's formation in 1944, accepted the post of Australian High Commissioner in London in 1956.

Menzies addressed a meeting of Liberal members and senators on the Suez crisis before they turned to the matter of electing Harrison's successor on 26 September 1956. The discussion on Suez was designed to highlight Menzies' disapproval of Richard Casey's approach to the crisis as Minister for External Affairs and to weaken his chances of becoming Deputy Leader. There were four candidates: Philip McBride, Bill Spooner, Dick Casey and Harold Holt. The press speculated that McBride and Spooner would be quickly eliminated. Political commentator Ron Watson thought that Holt was 'closest to the man in the street. Younger than the others, he represented a departure from the crusted Toryism that was characteristic of the non-Labor parties pre-war. He could see the other fellow's point of view'.[43] John Bennetts of the *Age* newspaper thought Holt's performance 'in the industrial field – in which the Government's greatest blunders have occurred when his advice was ignored – and his administration of the Immigration portfolio show him to be Casey's superior as a politician and administrator'.[44] Most newspapers had tipped Casey to win. Others thought that Casey would succeed Menzies for a brief period before Holt assumed the prime ministership. This would give Casey an opportunity for national leadership and Holt more time to gain experience. In its analysis of the close result, the *Canberra Times* claimed there had been 'a set against Mr Holt by some elements within his party on the very opposite grounds to those which commend him in national affairs. He has been attacked because he has sought to maintain the immigration programme, and he has been criticised by those on his side of politics who believe he is too close to labour'.[45] Holt was victorious and most considered him Menzies' natural successor.

As the Federal Opposition was divided and dispirited after the party's catastrophic split in 1955 with anti-communist members forming the Democratic Labor Party (DLP), Holt believed the Government should work even harder to demonstrate its unity and capacity for vision. With its immediate electoral future assured, 'it would be stupid of us to lapse into complacency'. Holt noted the tendency of the Australian electorate to turn against the Government without being convinced that the alternative was better while Labor polled well despite internal upheavals. He wanted a new appeal to be made to the Australian people. The Liberal Party had successfully secured much of the middle class. It now needed to broaden its appeal and bolster elector loyalty. Holt remarked:

> We still lack a sufficiently large following of devoted people who are wholeheartedly for our principles, and enthusiastic about the way we apply them. We have been 'delivering the goods' in terms of sustained prosperity, development and full employment. We are generally regarded as being 'sounder' on national finance, foreign relations and defence. We have managed to attract enough 'marginal voters' of the artisan, farmer, small shopkeeper type, etc., to ensure our parliamentary majority. But we have never experienced the fervour and unquestioning loyalty which Labour

[sic] could confidently expect for so many of its better years from a great mass of people. We have yet to face the challenge of bad seasons, growing unemployment, or a unified Labour Movement under a more popular leadership.[46]

Holt suggested that the only two major national initiatives of the post-war period, the Snowy Mountains project and large-scale immigration, actually originated with the Labor Party. According to Holt the Government still lacked 'imagination' and the public's support was fickle. The Coalition parties needed 'a story likely to arouse some enthusiasm towards us from the public'. He wanted to transcend electoral popularity in reaching for philosophical commitment. The central elements of the story were industrial expansion and mineral exploration tied together 'as examples of what is going on in this country, during a period when it is being soundly governed in accordance with Liberal principles'. But he also recognised that Australian liberalism had 'so individualised political allegiance, framing citizens as responsible to themselves, their families and their workplaces, that this allowed little vision of a national story'.[47]

When he succeeded Arthur Fadden as Treasurer in December 1958, Holt's capacity to develop policy was constrained. His role was to increase public revenues and decrease public spending while ensuring the government did not take too much or return too little to the people. As Treasurer he was more the facilitator of policy that its initiator although he worked to establish the Reserve Bank of Australia and to introduce decimal currency. Holt was personally involved in selecting designs for the new notes and coins. He led the public campaign to explain the new system and promote the inclusion of Australian designs on the coins and the use of different colours for the notes, convincing his colleagues that the 'dollar' was preferable to the 'royal' as the name of the new banknote. The Treasury did not suit Holt's temperament. He was reluctant to intervene in the economy when the consequences of Government action could not be confidently predicted or tightly controlled. His eventual efforts to ease inflation resulted in the 1961 credit squeeze known as 'Holt's jolt'. For the first time in his political career, Holt's judgement was questioned. The portfolio was, in many respects, too technical for his usual approach to public administration because he was often left with little room for manoeuvre. But Holt survived and the economy returned to growth by 1965. His Cabinet seniority required him to serve in the portfolio; his instincts told him the job was not a good fit for his disposition.

The liberal prime minister

When Sir Robert Menzies retired in January 1966, all eyes turned to his long-serving party deputy. Holt appealed to the broadest sentiments of the Liberal Party. He had not been associated with any particular group or faction in the organisation. Within the Party there had always been tension between its upper-middle class old money members and the middle class business and professional people. Stanley Bruce and Richard Casey were representative of the former; Harold Holt and John Gorton of the latter.

From his first election to parliament in 1935, Holt's inclinations and sympathies were those of the political centre. He did not attempt to change his political persona on becoming prime minister. He was still a pragmatist rather than a philosopher but continued to claim a lineage connecting him with Alfred Deakin and approvingly quoted his political mantra that 'we are liberal always, radical often and reactionary never'. In noting the conditions of change and continuity that prevailed in his prime ministership compared with the situation facing Deakin half a century earlier, Holt claimed that there has

> inevitably to be change in emphasis according

to the needs of the times. There are today issues of great importance to the nation which occupy the attention of politicians but they are not of a nature that attracts radicals nor do they call for radical thinking in the terms of these early years of federation ... New systems and methods of communication between the politician and the public have changed our habits and the tasks which fall on Ministers and backbenchers alike. But the old values remain. It is because of the very fact of our pledge to political liberty and individual freedom that we can absorb change and maintain our identity.[48]

Holt's preference for maximising his political scope for policy and action accounted for his dislike of the Treasury portfolio. Like most other political leaders of his day, Holt did not come to the nation's highest elected office with a comprehensive vision for Australia or an agenda for wholesale political, economic, social or diplomatic reform or restructure other than a program of 'taking Australia into Asia' – as he described it. Rather, he was committed to preserving a certain approach to public policy and a specific mood in public discourse.

The principles which attracted me to the Liberal Party in the first instance are a truly Australian outlook, a determination to preserve for the Australian people freedom for the individual, opportunities and incentives for the individual, with emphasis on freedom of the individual. These things have endured throughout the life of the party, and I believe these principles are the reason why we are attracting at this time so many young people either to our ranks or to our political support.[49]

Holt believed that public demands shaped public policy. This meant that politicians need 'in-built radar systems which will sense when something he proposes is likely to have serious electoral repercussions'.[50] Thus, he was not an innovator but a searcher after consensus long before the term became synonymous with Bob Hawke's prime ministership. He commented: 'In this country the margins for movement are not very great and the politician must judge as accurately as he can the likely impact of his policies upon public opinion if he wishes to retain office'.[51] Consequently, he did not intend to embark on an ambitious legislative program or attempt major constitutional change (although he was one of few prime ministers to sponsor a successful referendum). In fact, his only detailed statement on the status and standing of the Constitution would be a foreword to Justice Percy Joske's *Australian Federal Government*.

The existence of a written constitution has affected the political, economic and social life of the Australian people less than is generally supposed. While in Australia neither the national nor any one of the state governments is individually in the position of exercising full legal sovereignty over the whole field of government, this very fact has encouraged a spirit of active cooperation and partnership. This process has become increasingly evident in recent years. There is less disposition in the present than in the past on the part of Commonwealth governments to look for new heads of power which might be employed without being unduly troubled by the attitudes of the state governments. The reluctance of the electorate to make changes in the Constitution is well recognised and, in modern times, resort is made to consultation and conference discussion between heads of governments or the ministers appropriate to particular subject matters … One of the traditional objections in British thinking to the existence of a written constitution that might prove difficult to amend is the fear that it will prevent governments from meeting the known wishes of the people as changing circumstances occur. Australian experience has been otherwise … successive administrations have been responsive to the needs of the time, and that, with rare exceptions, the Constitution has not proved an insurmountable barrier.[52]

This led some to be critical of Holt's capacity for compromise and his alleged tendency towards opportunism. In a savage attack on the new prime minister, an editorial in the *Australian Financial Review* criticised Holt for his lack of philosophical convictions and political commitments: 'The most outstanding characteristic of Holt's politics is their elusiveness. Unkindly one could say that he was a plasticine man – imprinted with the philosophy, beliefs, arguments of the last person with whom he came in contact'.[53] This was grossly unfair but it highlighted the need for Holt to declare firmly the things for which he and his government stood that would set him and them apart from the previous administrations. As someone who maintained the discipline of confining himself to matters within his own portfolio, he had some deep and creative thinking to do in terms of a domestic agenda.

Holt's leadership style was to guide Cabinet towards a consensus consistent with the Party's philosophy and the practical needs of the nation. He explained his approach shortly after becoming Prime Minister: 'Leadership can take various forms. There is the type of leadership which is so far out in front of the team that there is danger of lack of cooperation, lack of warmth and some loss of effectiveness. There is the leadership which can lead but, at the same time, be close enough to the team to be part of it and be on the basis of friendly cooperation. I will make that my technique of leadership'.[54] Holt also wanted to distinguish between his role within Cabinet and his office as national leader and public perceptions of both.

> I don't think we get from the public, as yet anyhow,
> the veneration which apparently develops around a
> President of the United States. The Prime Minister
> here is very much in the firing line of political
> action. The events of recent years are tending
> to accentuate this because the publicity media –
> [television] particularly, the press and radio – all
> tend to concentrate attention these days on the
> head of government, and whereas sitting around
> the cabinet table he should be regarded as the first
> among equals, in the eyes of the public he tends
> to be regarded as, not only the leading figure, but
> virtually a dominant figure in the administration.[55]

Holt was, therefore, thoroughly collaborative in his
approach, taking Cabinet through each submission
page-by-page or even line-by-line if necessary. Each
member was given a chance to comment and to be
part of the decision-making although it was frequently
long and tortuous. Holt's problem was trying to satisfy
everyone or, at least, attempting to accommodate
competing viewpoints. As political scientists Clem
Lloyd and Gordon Reid note: '[Holt] observed the
conventions of the Cabinet system of government as
developed in Australia. He viewed himself as chairman
of a committee, the first among equals, vested with
the responsibility of giving leadership but where the
consensus of Cabinet opinion was clearly against him,
the instrument and executor of the majority decision'.[56]
Because Holt had been 'an equal' for so long, it was not

surprising that parliamentary colleagues like Ian Sinclair thought of the new Prime Minister as a 'colleague and a partner'. Cabinet members soon realised that Holt could be quite determined, occasionally to the point of obstinacy, while he was rarely deflected from the agreed course of action. Yet, he did not feel the need to speak on every issue as Menzies had done nor did he have an ambitious legislative program. It was perhaps for this reason that he did not direct his ministers to be more disciplined in their Cabinet submissions.

During his first major address to the Liberal Party in February 1966, Holt was keen to emphasise that the Party was not synonymous with Sir Robert Menzies; that it had an organisation which had accounted for its electoral success as much as his predecessor's leadership. It was a young party that developed its own customs and traditions that had given it stability and vitality. Furthermore,

> Australia has need of the Liberal Party. We had reached [in 1944] a point in our affairs when we needed a party which would stand for all sections of the Australian community, which would cast aside, once and for all, the old bitter concept of class warfare, the struggle between employer and employee; that would see in the needs of Australia a need for a party of unity, a party which could develop a co-operating democracy with the Parliaments of the States; not trying to make Federation work by imposing authority from the

> centre or by so construing the Federal powers that
> the States were reduced to nothingness, but a true
> Federation based upon a spirit of cooperation
> rather than on a strict definition of powers.[57]

In seeking to differentiate itself from Labor and the '36 faceless men' of the ALP Federal Executive, the Liberal Party wanted to stress

> Our Council is not a council of Party bosses. If
> we reach conclusions about Federal policy, we send
> them to the Government as recommendations.
> We don't give orders to the Government. We
> don't make policy for the Government and don't
> compel the Government to carry it out. It is our
> belief that the final responsibility for policy rests
> with the Government elected by, and responsible
> to, voters.[58]

Given the pace of social change and cultural transition, the Liberal Party would need to draw on its philosophical foundations and think imaginatively about nationhood and national symbols. With the sun rapidly setting on the British Empire, Holt told the Young Australian Foundation at the University of Melbourne that whereas the nation once looked to Britain and the Royal Navy, 'we have now realised that Australia is a national independent entity of its own and that Australia faces problems and has obligations which are quite unlike anything the earlier generations of Australian had to meet'.[59] The unifying symbols of Crown, religion and race were disintegrating. But what would replace them? Perhaps ideals and virtues common to civilised societies that were not dependent on a particular nationality or a specific ethnicity?

Holt was willing to lead but did not always seem sure about the direction. His liberalism appeared to offer few answers at times and his imagination seemed to have evaporated. The almost indecipherable handwritten notes that were the basis of some of his speeches on these matters bordered on incoherent. They were a grab-bag of subjects and themes mixed with second thoughts and adjoining arrows to suggest a logical flow of ideas that plainly did not exist in the Prime Minister's mind. No-one should have been surprised when Holt said that 'if we're going anywhere, we're not going American, we're going Australian, and there is, I think, a stronger sense of nationalism, a growing feeling of pride in Australia, its achievements, its potentialities, even its hazards'.[60] The Prime Minister hoped the people would provide a lead even as he emphasised the importance of harmony and homogeneity in the meantime.

In any event, Holt believed, prescribing national identity was not a task undertaken by Government or the Prime Minister. National unity would arise from the common life of the people; they would be drawn together by those things in which they felt a common destiny. As Prime Minister, he said, 'it is my responsibility to reflect the modern Australia to my fellow countrymen, to our Allies and the outside world at large'.[61] He continued to believe there were limits to government intervention and areas of public life into which it ought not to stray either because it had no mandate or no competence. When government focussed on social policy it ought to reflect community aspirations rather than dictate them. Here Holt looked to the 'forgotten people', the moral middle class he had inherited from Menzies, whose mood and mind he claimed to understand. He had long believed that 80 per cent of the electorate would invariably vote Liberal or Labor. This left 20 per cent of the voters who would make or break the Government. Holt believed they still coincided with the 'forgotten people' and he made them his main focus. What could he say or do that would attract and retain their votes? Compromise and consensus would be sought to yield the answer.

At a party rally in Melbourne, Holt reiterated his understanding of the Liberal Party's platform and emphasised its four pillars: a positive philosophy of freedom, enhancing opportunities for freedom, encouraging incentive for effort and ensuring a minimum of state interference with daily life. His Government would maintain a policy of full employment and promote national growth through major infrastructure projects and immigration.[62] What kinds of new arrivals would Australia accept? It was not surprising that Holt turned quickly to a field in which he had already achieved notable success – immigration – to demonstrate the shift in social policy he wanted to promote. In his first official statement as prime minister, broadcast on national television on 20 February 1966, Holt foreshadowed a change to Australia's immigration policy to allow for 'more flexibility … [and] a spirit of humanity' particularly in relation to non-European migration. The changes being proposed would go further than those of the previous decade because, Holt argued, the 'White Australia Policy' (as it was called in the Liberal Party platform until removed in 1960 and the Labor platform until 1965), was an international embarrassment and a problem for Australia's external relations.[63] But he assured the electorate that this 'did not mean fundamentals of the restrictive policy would be changed'.[64] In fact, this is exactly what the changes would bring about and Holt knew it. He needed to calm community fears while making changes that would serve the national interest. Holt dealt with the anxiety and offered a better future.

For the greatest part, he found the job of prime minister more reactive than proactive. He was confronted by the continuing routine business of government and a succession of real and purported national crises. Although the economy was buoyant, business and trade union leaders were disappointed that

Holt's first statement on economic matters was neither imaginative nor creative. There was evidence of a slight increase in unemployment, real wages were declining, housing approvals were down and the growth in gross domestic product was minimal. Sections of the media noted that Australia's 'stop-go' economy had 'come to a Holt'. While business wanted the Government to stimulate economic growth, the ACTU asked the Government to consider the needs of pensioners and social security recipients. Although the new Treasurer, William McMahon, showed he was willing to dispute and reject departmental advice, Holt was disinclined to initiate a major Government spending program for fear of increasing inflation. When rising costs caused problems for major projects like the Ord River Scheme and the Mount Newman mine, Commonwealth investment was on the lower end of expectation. The same was true of drought relief. The persistence of a severe drought that began in 1965 occupied Holt's first few weeks in office and provided a chance to accumulate some goodwill with his Coalition partner. Holt said that Commonwealth financial assistance 'would cover whatever deficit [the States] might have in their budget as a result of drought relief measures their Governments might take'.[65] A month later[66] he announced the establishment of a new system of farm loans. The scheme would cost $50 million and 'provide primary producers with greater access to medium and long term finance through the banking system for farm development purposes, including measures for drought recovery and mitigation of future droughts'.[67] But he was criticised by various lobby groups for giving too little too late. It appeared in relation to the economy that reticence was mistaken for liberalism and caution was overcoming imagination. Holt was too concerned with unexpected outcomes and unintended consequences.

Holt faced the electorate and their verdict on his brief administration in November 1966. His performance had been good rather than great. The Government's successes outnumbered its failures. The Prime Minister delivered a pre-recorded policy speech for television and radio two weeks before the poll. The message and the medium reflected the aphorism that oppositions do not win elections; governments lose them. The Liberal Party's approach was long on caution and short on imagination. The policy launch was a tightly controlled event and confined to the issue of 'external security coupled with a forward-looking domestic program'. The Liberal Party organisation had earlier told the Prime Minister that 'Great Debates' between the main party leaders had 'no positive vote-winning value and should be avoided if possible'.[68] A decision had also been made to avoid the main policy speech being delivered at a public meeting because it 'would involve serious risk of demonstration and interruption' largely because of opposition to Australian involvement in the war in South Vietnam. Described by a *Sydney Morning Herald* media commentator as a 'recitation', Holt had clearly 'been over and over his lines so that he used the teleprompter rarely. His voice was expressionless and utterly without force. The script was so crammed that the most ardent Liberal could not digest a fraction of it'.[69] Holt's speech was long on the familiar anti-communist rhetoric but short on details of how and when the escalating war in South Vietnam would be won. On the domestic front, Holt said the Government would create a new ministry of education and science; allocate funds for new teacher training colleges; double grants to independent schools for the building of science blocks; ease the means testing of pensions; increase investment in water conservation projects; expand research in the wool industry; and establish an Australian Tourist Commission.

The Government was re-elected with an unexpected record majority. Holt had secured his own mandate to govern and had shown the Liberal Party could be electorally successful without its founder. In most respects, 1967 was a repeat of the previous year with a steady stream of new but relatively modest policy initiatives. The most lasting achievement of that year was the referendum held on 27 May 1967. Two questions were put to the Australian people. The first related to increasing the size of the House of Representatives without enlarging the Senate. It was defeated. The second referendum question was designed to remove discriminatory clauses in the Constitution relating to Aborigines. [70]

On assuming office as Prime Minister in early 1966, Holt was advised that this proposal might not receive majority support. The referendum was originally to have been put to the people in 1965 but was delayed with Menzies' retirement and the conduct of a Federal election in November 1966. The original 'Yes' case proposed by Menzies in 1965 was limited to removing section 127 of the Constitution which stated: 'In reckoning the numbers of the people of the Commonwealth, or of a State or other part of the Commonwealth, aboriginal natives shall not be counted'. He said this was 'completely out of harmony with our national attitudes'.[71] The Federal Council for the Advancement of Aborigines and Torres Strait Islanders (FCAATSI) also wanted the phrase 'other than the aboriginal race in any State' deleted from section 51 (xxvi) to empower the Commonwealth to legislate specifically on their behalf, especially in preventing discrimination against Aborigines in the States. Prime Minister Menzies believed this was not an exclusion from equal rights but a protection against the Commonwealth making laws that discriminated against Aborigines. There was, he believed, no need to amend section 51 (xxvi). But Labor's Gordon Bryant argued that the Commonwealth cannot 'possibly take up the challenge in respect of Aborigines unless it takes to itself the power to do so'.[72] Menzies did not, however, favour direct Commonwealth involvement in Aboriginal affairs as he was not convinced that the Commonwealth would be any more effective than the States in delivering social services or combating community problems. By this time, legislation had already (1962) been enacted to give Aborigines the right to vote in Federal elections[73] with Queensland the last State to do so in 1965. The Commonwealth had also been involved in Aboriginal affairs in the Northern Territory since 1911 and could, although legal opinion was equivocal, have played a role within the States through the provisions of section 96 of the Constitution which probably allowed the Commonwealth to make grants to the States on such terms and conditions as it sees fit.

The advice that Holt received in relation to section 51 (xxvi) was that the extant wording was not discriminatory; that adding a new provision invalidating any Commonwealth or State discrimination on the grounds of race would prompt litigation; that the best protection for Aborigines was to treat them for all purposes as though they were Australian citizens; and, that inserting a third matter in the referendum might militate against a 'yes' vote. Aboriginal leaders felt, however, that leaving section 51 unchanged could mean that Aborigines were the only racial group mentioned in the Constitution and give the impression they were infants unable to manage their own affairs. Aboriginal advocates firmly believed it was necessary for the Commonwealth to be able to legislate for the benefit of Aborigines on a national basis.[74] Holt was, however, persuaded that that both sections of the Constitution should be changed 'because they have been widely misinterpreted' and because there was 'a general impression that they are discriminatory' although the Government nonetheless regarded this opinion as erroneous.[75] Holt announced the successful passage through Parliament of the Constitution Alteration Bills on 14 March 1967 with the changes to both sections of the Constitution put in one question to the electorate rather than two. Holt made no firm undertakings to use the additional legislative power the referendum would deliver to the Government although the press made it clear that the success of the 'Yes' vote would deny the Commonwealth any excuse for not doing more for Aborigines. A 'No' case was never formulated, never printed and never circulated.

On one level, Holt was deeply distressed by the need for the referendum. As a former immigration minister who had welcomed people of many different nationalities to this country, he was not convinced that Australia had the serious race problems he had observed elsewhere. He was unable to see beyond his own attitudes which he sincerely believed were free from racism. While conceding that there were 'occasional and unrelated acts of discrimination' reported from time to time, he asserted that they were dealt with once publicised. And where there was discrimination, it would end once 'the habits, manners and education of the race more nearly approached general community standards'. In the mind of Holt and most of his colleagues at that time, Aborigines could participate in Australia's public life but they had to think and act like Europeans. Historian John Hirst was right when he observed that Holt was 'more concerned about Australia's image in the world and wanted to show that he was sympathetic to the Aboriginal cause'.[76] But at the same time he did not want to 'magnify the Aborigine problem out of its true reality'.[77] On the eve of the referendum Holt said: 'anything but a yes vote to this question would do injury to our reputation among fair-minded people everywhere'.[78]

As the first referendum question revealed, bi-partisan support for the 'Yes' case was no guarantee of success notwithstanding a large and vigorous community campaign. On the second referendum question the 'Yes' vote was carried in every State with a national majority of 90.77 per cent. This was despite some last minute anxieties within the Aboriginal community. More than five million Australians had voted in favour of constitutional change. It was, and remains, the most successful referendum in Australian political history. It was followed by calls for immediate Commonwealth action including creation of a new Commonwealth department. Holt made a statement en route to Europe about the results. He was disappointed by the nexus question, being surprised that 'the majority of voters chose to ignore the advice of those to whom they normally look for guidance on political matters'. As for the question on aborigines, he said the strong result 'will contribute to Australia's international standing by demonstrating to the outside world our overwhelming desire to give full acceptance to the aboriginal people within our community'.[79] Holt could now confidently claim that Australia was not a racist country. But he continued to promote the importance of assimilation despite allegations that it was intended to eliminate aboriginality and Aboriginal culture. In his view, 'it may be that this will happen but if it does it is a matter of individual decision and not of policy'.[80]

While Holt expressed no doubts publicly about the likely referendum result, former diplomat Barrie Dexter recalls that Holt was privately astonished by the obvious strength of feeling. In fact, '[Holt] had not really expected the referendum to succeed. When it did, and so overwhelmingly, he realised that there was something about the electorate which he, as a politician who prided himself on interpreting the public mood, had not understood. He was determined to come to grips with this, and to achieve what the people so clearly wanted – strong Commonwealth leadership'.[81]

But no specific plans had been made and Holt was under pressure not to develop any. The Aboriginal Welfare Conference of State and Commonwealth Ministers held in Perth in July 1967 voted for a preservation of the status quo with the Victorian Minister for Aboriginal Welfare arguing that 'uniform Commonwealth legislation would be a retrograde step'.[82] Holt initially agreed: 'there is a big variation in circumstances and needs of Aborigines in the States. For this reason, administration has to be on a regional or State basis if it is to be effective'.[83] But he soon realised Commonwealth coordination was vital and his liberal instincts and political imagination had deserted him. Holt visited Aboriginal communities, met leading indigenous spokesmen like Charles Perkins, and read whatever he could obtain on Aboriginal history and culture. Bill (WC) Wentworth had earlier suggested that Perkins might convene an 'Aboriginal Advisory Panel'.[84]

Having firmly committed the Commonwealth to leadership in Aboriginal affairs and realising this was an opportunity to be imaginative, Holt established a three-member Council for Aboriginal Affairs on 2 November 1967. Its role was to 'advise the Government in the formulation of national policies for the advancement of the Aboriginal citizens of Australia ... and to provide the machinery necessary for joint consultation as the need arises with the States and with relevant

Commonwealth departments'.[85] Its members would
be Dr HC 'Nugget' Coombs (who would shortly
retire from the governorship of the Reserve Bank),
Barrie Dexter and Australian National University
social anthropologist, Professor WEH 'Bill' Stanner.[86]
Coombs, was prepared to join the Council and to act
as its chairman only after Holt 'assured me that it was
his firm intention to use the new Commonwealth
powers genuinely to transform the status and welfare
of Aborigines and his actions gave evidence of his
sincerity in that undertaking'.[87] Dexter was made
Executive Member of the Council and Director of
the Office of Aboriginal Affairs which was created to
service the council. Stanner, a senior academic at the
Australian National University, only consented to join
the Council because Coombs and Dexter had already
agreed to become members. Stanner was impressed by
Holt's personal interest and commitment to aboriginal
people. He was assured that the prime minister
intended to take personal responsibility for aboriginal
affairs by locating an Office of Aboriginal Affairs
within his Department and to use the authority of his
position to implement the Council's policy initiatives.
Bill Wentworth, a long-time advocate for indigenous
people who was later appointed Minister-in-Charge
of Aboriginal Affairs, urged Holt to expedite action
as 'our supporters in the Aboriginal field are being
whittled away from us and humiliated by reason of

delay in practical Commonwealth initiative'.[88]

What was behind Holt's commitment to advancing indigenous affairs? Coombs believed that he 'turned to initiatives in the Arts and for Aborigines' because his Government 'lacked major agreed tasks or objectives to unify the energies of its ministers and supporters'. He also believed that these two areas 'better expressed his own generous and human spirit'.[89] Whatever Holt's reasons, and genuine concern and empathy were certainly among them, he had taken the initiative and shown his determination to improve the wellbeing of Aboriginal people. Holt had approached Coombs about other areas of public service he might render. Reflecting his life-long interest in theatre and ballet, Holt was open to Coombs' persuasion that the arts in Australia needed a government agency broader than the Australian Elizabethan Theatre Trust. Late in 1967, he established an Australian Council for the Arts under Coombs direction and gave it the task of coordinating policies on government support.

Holt initiated other important policies in his second year as prime minister. In May 1967, he floated the idea of ending appeals from the High Court to the Privy Council in matters of Federal jurisdiction. It met with widespread support but some disapproval within the Liberal Party Federal Council.[90] Sir Garfield Barwick, the Chief Justice of the High Court, told

Holt that he supported the move because he felt that Australia needed to make its own legal mistakes. In September 1967 the Government formally announced its intentions although the abolition of Privy Council appeals did not become law until 6 August 1968. Holt had earlier written to Prime Minister Harold Wilson to explain that there was nothing in the timing which was so close to his publicly stated disappointment with Britain's decision to withdraw its forces east of Suez. He said: 'we regard the decision as a desirable expression of national maturity, and I am sure that you will so recognise it'.[91] He also wanted to relocate the statue of King George V from King's Hall in Parliament House and remove the memorial to the former monarch situated at the front of the building.[92] There was some substance to these symbolic gestures.

Over the weekend of 16-17 December 1967, Holt discussed the prospect of a major European tour to 'sell' the possibilities and potentialities of Asia with his press secretary Tony Eggleton. He wanted to elucidate and explain the security dilemmas being faced by its emerging democracies. Holt believed that during his previous visits 'it became clear that Australia has been accepted as a member of the Asian and Pacific community. We are not on the outside looking in, but we are regarded as one of the countries of the area, involved in its problems'.[93] Holt had already achieved much in the field of diplomacy and foreign policy.

He strived to have Australians think more creatively about trading with Asia and helped them to overcome historic fears and anxieties. He met most of South East Asia's leaders and tried to convince them that Australia wanted to play a constructive and positive part in regional affairs while he worked to overcome the residual effects of the White Australia Policy. He deserved credit for both his willingness to tackle the problems and for building closer relations with Australia's nearer neighbours.

On Sunday 17 December 1967, Holt entered the water at Cheviot Beach and was swept out to sea. His body was never recovered. A memorial service was held in St Paul's Cathedral at Melbourne five days later. It was the largest gathering of world leaders in Australian history. Harold Holt had been Prime Minister for 692 days – not long enough to secure a place among the ranks of great Australian national leaders.

A liberal legacy

The *Australian Financial Review* gathered a panel of six historians[94] to rate Australia's best and worst prime ministers as part of a series of retrospectives commemorating the Centenary of Federation in 2001.[95] Each historian was asked to nominate five incumbents in each category. The range of opinion reflected their own political leanings. Only Alfred Deakin featured in each historian's 'best' list while Sir William McMahon appeared in five of six 'worst' lists. Holt did not appear in any of the 'best' lists but was nominated twice in the 'worst' list – those of Stuart MacIntyre and Clem Lloyd. Both are well known for their Left-leaning political sympathies. After Deakin, who was easily ahead of other contenders for the best prime minister, were Sir Robert Menzies, John Curtin, Ben Chifley and Gough Whitlam. Behind McMahon were James Scullin, George Reid, Joseph Cook with Harold Holt ranking alongside Stanley Melbourne Bruce. Their reasons for placing Holt on the 'worst' list were not disclosed. The *Sydney Morning Herald* remarked: 'At least he will be remembered as one of the most likeable of Australian prime ministers'.[96] This was certainly the view of his colleagues.

In explaining why Holt will never be numbered among the great Australian prime ministers, his inability to manage power and deal with opposition – both within and beyond his own party – looms largest. The efficient use of power and the effective exercise of leadership require particular character traits and a cause or purpose to which they are directed. The absence of vital traits and the failure to articulate specific goals meant that greatness would probably always elude Harold Holt. As the publicist Edgar Holt observed, Harold saw 'all people through rose-tinted spectacles. He seemed quite incapable of saying an unkind word about anybody. In the whole of Canberra it would be difficult to discover a man who ever recalled hearing Holt say anything personally hurtful. This, in itself, made him unique'.[97] His dislike for acrimony and his yearning for affection meant he was 'the nicest man Australia had as a Prime Minister, but his very niceness was a major factor in his political failure … Holt was too unsure of himself, too lacking in the intellectual qualities needed for the making of major decisions, ever to be more than a good 'departmental' man.[98]

These assessments only partly explain the disappointment of Harold Holt's prime ministership. Holt never conceived an inspiring vision of what Australia might become under his leadership. This is surprising given he served in Parliament for three decades before becoming prime minister in 1966 and was clearly the heir apparent from 1956. It was not that he thought a liberal outlook prevented him from embracing such a vision. While Holt recognised that Australia was changing and that the times demanded a new kind of political leadership, it was his increasing conventionality and conformity that prevented him from thinking creatively or expansively about what the country could become with imaginative and generous leadership. His enthusiasm for change subsided alongside his bohemian tastes as middle age tempered his openness to diversity. In sum, his creativity and imagination were dissipated as he was gradually institutionalised in a public life more preoccupied with management than leadership, processes ahead of possibilities. This may have simply been a function of advancing age but I am not persuaded. In part, he lost his nerve.

While the electorate appeared to want the same of what they had enjoyed under Menzies when they went to the polls to re-elect the Holt Government in November 1966, by the latter part of 1967 the mood had shifted and younger voters seemed either bored or impatient with the Coalition's 'grey men'. Holt could not rely on politics being 'business as usual'. The 'forgotten people', the moral middle class Holt had inherited from Menzies, were being transformed into what Judith Brett has referred to as the 'chattering classes and the chardonnay set, self-interested minorities and cosmopolitan elites'. They were moving from being concerned Liberal voters to forming the progressive Left.[99]

The decline of the liberal imagination

As human beings mature and life experiences inform values and shape virtues, there will be slow and perhaps imperceptible changes to an individual's sense of identity and destiny. Deepened self-awareness and altered perceptions of what matters will be reflected in an evolving philosophy of life. Harold Holt's political outlook changed steadily over three decades of public service. Youthful idealism gave way to practical realism by the time he was aged forty and appointed to the portfolios of Immigration and Labour and National Service in 1949. From his brief ministerial service in 1940-41, Holt started to recognise the limits of government intervention and the rigidities of public administration. Experience tempered the exercise of imagination alongside close and continuing encounters with public servants who identified weakness in his ideas and optimism in his initiatives. He was wiser but not without hope that government could contribute to human happiness. Throughout eight years of parliamentary opposition from 1941-1949, he had never succumbed to cynicism of parliamentary processes nor allowed himself the luxury of feeling contempt for the electorate. But the uncertain condition of the economy and the turbulent nature of political competition had tempered his belief in what the state should attempt and could achieve. What remained was a sincere commitment to liberalism and the need to think creatively about what a better future demanded of legislators.

I hadn't noticed the consistency of his liberalism when writing his biography more than a decade ago. Nor had I appreciated that his political philosophy encouraged, if not required, the consistent exercise of imagination. Eschewing the rigidities of both conservatism and communism, Holt was obliged to address each policy challenge on its own merits and without the intrusion of a prescriptive creed demanding specific outcomes regardless of whether they were efficient or effective. A man of genuinely liberal instincts, he pre-judged few issues and arrived at conclusions that frequently frustrated more conservative colleagues in the Liberal Party. He was, for instance, keenly aware of the dangers of agricultural and industrial protectionism and the need for Australian primary producers and manufacturers to be prepared for greater global competition before they become financially non-viable. Holt was unpersuaded by the claim that government monopolies needed to be preserved or that the economy needed close political management. His liberal instincts made him perennially wary of most forms of government intervention. Not only was he opposed to authoritarianism, he acknowledged the limits of the state's administrative competence and never believed that politicians and bureaucrats knew what was best for individuals and their families. Deciding when and how the government ought to act was crucial to the liberal imagination that marked his political life. While it looked from time to time as though he was indecisive, it was a reflection of the reticence embedded in his political credo, to recall David Kemp's description of political convictions. In 1966, the electorate preferred Holt's promotion of a liberal agenda and individualist ideas to the socialism and collectivist ideas championed by Opposition Leader Arthur Calwell. Holt had secured the largest parliamentary majority in Australian history but failed to use the electorate's strong endorsement to innovate across a range of portfolios. Having secured a mandate, he seemed more interested in preserving than applying it.

Holt would have been a better prime minister had he been less afraid of failure. In contrast to one of his successors, Gough Whitlam, who seemed indifferent to the possibility that he might fail and who was disinterested in the consequences of such failure, Holt erred too much on the side of caution. But his brief prime ministership left a lasting legacy in the areas of immigration, aboriginal affairs, regional trade, legal reform and the arts. They remain tributes to his ability to manage change while assuaging fears and promoting hope, and show what the exercise of a liberal imagination can deliver for a country experiencing transition.

ENDNOTES

1   David Kemp, 'Leadership Practices: Reflections on Australian Political Leadership', pp. 203-216 in Paul 't Hart and John Uhr (eds), *Public Leadership: Perspectives and Practices*, ANU E-Press, Canberra, 2008, pp. 206-207 quoted.

2   Kemp, 'Leadership Practices', p. 213.

3   Lyndon B Johnson, 'The President's Prologue and Epilogue to 'This America'', 3 October 1966. Available online at Gerhard Peters and John T Woolley, *The American Presidency Project*, http://www.presidency.ucsb.edu/ws/?pid=27900.

4   Arthur Fadden, *They Call Me Artie*, Jacaranda, Brisbane, 1969, p. 149.

5   Commonwealth Parliamentary Debates (hereafter CPD) (Reps), 27 March 1941, pp. 338-40.

6   *Australian Women's Weekly*, 15 March 1941.

7   *Telegraph* (Sydney), 8 August 1942.

8   *Mercury* (Hobart), 12 March 1945.

9   *Daily News* (Perth) Monday 30 July 1945.

10 'Causes of Industrial Unrest', Opening Lecture, Winter Forum of the Australian Institute of Political Science', 3 July 1946, Federation Hall, Sydney, National Archives of Australia (hereafter NAA), M 2607 1.

11 SMH, 15 September 1949.

12 *Age*, 4 October 1949.

13 *Sun* (Sydney), 12 November 1949.

14 *Herald* (Melbourne), 23 November 1949.

15 *Herald* (Melbourne), 6 December 1949.

16 *Smith's Weekly*, 7 January 1950.

17 *Herald* (Melbourne), 23 December 1949.

18 Address to the Australian Citizenship Convention, Canberra, 24 January 1950.

19 Robert Murray, *The Split: Australian Labor in the Fifties*, Hale & Iremonger, Sydney, 1984, p. 145.

20   Don Watson, *Brian Fitzpatrick: A Radical Life*, Hale & Iremonger, Sydney, 1979, p. 234.

21   Geoffrey Bolton, *The Oxford History of Australia*, Oxford University Press, Melbourne, 1990, p. 77.

22   Alan Watt, *The Evolution of Australian Foreign Policy*, Cambridge, 1968, p. 202.

23   HI London, *Non-White Immigration and the 'White Australia' Policy*, Sydney University Press, Sydney, 1970, pp. 17-18.

24   *The Good Neighbour*, September 1956.

25   Jo Gullett, *In Good Company*, UQP, St Lucia, 1992, pp. 299-300.

26   Draft document headed 'Introduction', 7 February 1951, NAA M4299 3.

27   Alan Reid, *Sun* (Sydney), 15 May 1951.

28   *Age*, 28 October 1952.

29   *SMH*, 8 January 1954.

30   NAA M4299 2002/05179134 part 2.

31   *Mercury* (Hobart), 6 June 1957.

32   *Courier Mail* (Brisbane), 7 June 1957.

33   ILO Conference Proceedings, Thursday 27 June 1957.

34   'Training in Industry and Commerce: Proceedings of a One Day Conference, 24 June 1955', Australian Institute of Management, Adelaide Division. NAA M4299 2002/05179134 Part 4.

35   Don Whitington, *The Rulers: Fifteen Years of the Liberals*, revised edition, Cheshire-Lansdowne, Melbourne 1965, p. 76.

36   *Age*, 8 July 1952.

37   *Sun*, 1 July 1954.

38   Keith Sinclair, personal letter quoted in Broderick, BA (Hons) thesis, p. 8.

39   Blanche d'Alpuget, *Robert J Hawke: A Biography*, Lansdowne, Melbourne, 1982, p. 189.

40   *Daily Mirror* (Sydney), 20 January 1966.

41   'Suggested Lines of Government Policy', [undated but probably late

October or early November 1952], in 'General Internal Financial and Economic Policy 1952', NAA A571/135, Item 52/1161 Part 2.

42 *News* (Adelaide), 20 August 1954.

43 'Canberra Diary', *Voice*, May 1956.

44 'Canberra Commentary', *News* (Adelaide), 29 May 1956.

45 *Canberra Times*, 27 September 56.

46 Harold Holt, 'The Political Situation 4 February 1957', quoted in Ian Hancock, *National and Permanent?*, MUP, Melbourne, 2000, p. 169.

47 Murphy, *Imagining the Fifties*, Pluto Press, Sydney, 2000, p. 196.

48 Harold Holt, 'The Liberal Tradition in Australia – Alfred Deakin: His Life and Our Times', 1967 Alfred Deakin Lecture, in Yvonne Thompson, George Brandis and Tom Harley (eds), *Australian Liberalism: The Continuing Vision*, Liberal Forum Publication, 1986, pp. 83-84.

49 Holt, *Current Politics*, vol. 7, March 1966, p. 4.

50 *Age*, 21 January 1966.

51 ABC Radio Archives, Sydney, Tape reference: POL 86.

52 Foreword by Harold Holt to Justice Percy Joske, *Australian Federal Government*, First edition, Butterworths, Sydney, 1967.

53 *Australian Financial Review*, 21 January 1966, pp. 2-3.

54 Edgar Holt, *Politics is People: The Men of the Menzies Era*, Angus and Robertson, Sydney, 1969, p. 137.

55 Colin A Hughes, *Mr Prime Minister: Australian Prime Ministers 1901-1972*, Oxford University Press, Melbourne, 1976, p. 167.

56 Clem Lloyd & Gordon Reid, *Out of the Wilderness: The Return of Labor*, Cassell, Melbourne, 1974, p. 12-13.

57 Speech at a meeting in Box Hill, Victoria of the Liberal Party, 20 February 1966.

58 Jock Pagan, 'New Horizons in Liberal Thinking', address to the Liberal Party Federal Council, 4 September 1967.

59 Address to the Young Australian Convention, University of Melbourne, 11 March 1966.

60 Address to Royal Commonwealth Society luncheon, London, 8 September 1966.

61 Eastern Suburbs Liberal Rally, Box Hill Town Hall, 20 February 1966. M2684 125.

62 Eastern Suburbs Liberal Rally, Box Hill Town Hall, 20 February 1966. M2684 125.

63 Kenneth Rivett, *Australia and the Non-white Migrant*, MUP, Melbourne, 1975, pp. 25-29.

64 *SMH*, 21 February 1966.

65 Prime Ministerial Statement 17/1966 dated 23 February 1967, NAA M4295 21.

66 Prime Ministerial Statement 25/1966 dated 17 March 1966, NAA M4295 21.

67 CPD (Reps), 31 March 1966, p. 801.

68 'Minutes of the Meeting of the Federal Executive, 9 June 1966', NAA M2606 123.

69 *SMH*, 15 November 1966, press clipping, NAA M2684 134.

70 See PM's Department (CA 12) file, 'Constitution Alteration Bills – Procedure in Parliament and Referendum, 1965-1967', NAA A463, 1965/5445.

71 CPD (Reps), 11 November 1965, p. 2639.

72 CPD (Reps), 23 November 1965, p. 3072-4.

73 See Cabinet Secretariat (CA 3) file, 'Voting Rights for Aborigines – Policy, 1961-1962', NAA A4940, C3496.

74 See Faith Bandler, *Turning the Tide: A Personal History of the FCAATSI*, Aboriginal Studies Press, Canberra, 1989, p. 100-101.

75 Reported in the SMH, 28 February 1967.

76 John Hirst, *Australia's Democracy: A Short History*, Allen & Unwin, Sydney, 2002, p. 185.

77 NAA A 5482, 1-2; CPD (Reps) vol. 56, 7 September 1967, pp. 972-75.

78 Prime Ministerial Statement 54/1967 dated 26 May 1967, NAA M4295 21 Part 2.

79 Prime Ministerial Statement 55/1967, dated 28 May 1967, NAA M4295 Part 2.

80 CPD (Reps), 7 September 1967.

81 Barrie Dexter to author, 9 April 2001.

82 Quoted in FS Stevens (ed.), *Racism: The Australian Experience*, vol. 1, Sydney, 1971, p. 101.

83 Quoted in Margaret Ann Franklin, *Black and White Australians: An Inter-racial History, 1788-1975*, Heinemann, Melbourne, 1976, p. 189.

84 Wentworth to Holt, 3 October 1967, NAA M2684 135.

85 CPD (Reps), 7 September 1967, p. 973.

86 Prime Ministerial Statement 125/1967 dated 24 November 1967, NAA M4295 21 Part 2.

87 Coombs, *Trial Balance*, p. 270.

88 Wentworth to Holt, 23 November 1967, NAA M2684 135.

89 Coombs, *Trial Balance*, p. 270.

90 Minutes of the Meeting of the Federal Council of the Liberal Party, 4-5 September 1967, NAA M2606 123.

91 Holt to Wilson, 24 August 1967, NAA A7854 2.

92 These actions are referred to in a minute from McMahon to Holt, 30 March 1966, NAA M2606 116.

93 Christopher Forsyth, 'Australia (and Mr Holt) turn to Asia', *Australian*, 2 February 1967.

94 The panel consisted of Ian Hancock, Stuart MacIntyre, Graeme Davison, Geoffrey Bolton, Humphrey McQueen and Clem Lloyd.

95 Tony Walker and Jason Koutsoukis, 'The good, the bad and the couldabeens', *Australian Financial Review*, 3 January 2001, pp. 28-29.

96 *SMH*, 18 December 1967, p. 2.

97 Edgar Holt, *Politics is People*, p. 137.

98 Whitington, *Twelfth Man?*, pp. 117-18.

99 Judith Brett, *Australian Liberals and the Moral Middle Class: From Alfred Deakin to John Howard*, Cambridge University Press, Melbourne, 2003, pp. 210-11.

www.ingramcontent.com/pod-product-compliance
Lightning Source LLC
Chambersburg PA
CBHW060552100426
42742CB00013B/2528